KNOCK-KNOCK JOKES

By Mark Acey and Scott Nickel

Garfield created by JIM DAVIS

LERNER PUBLICATIONS ◆ MINNEAPOLIS

KNOCK, KNOCK.

Who's there?

Scott.

Scott who?

Scott a million of these jokes.

Lerner Publications Company
An imprint of Lerner Publishing Group, Inc.
241 First Avenue North
Minneapolis, MN 55401 USA

For reading levels and more information, look up this title at www.lernerbooks.com.

Main body text set in Mikado a.
Typeface provided by HVD fonts.

Editor: Allison Juda **Designer:** Susan Rouleau-Fienhage
Lerner team: Lauren Cooper and Sue Marquis

Library of Congress Cataloging-in-Publication Data

Names: Nickel, Scott, author. | Acey, Mark, author.
Title: Garfield's ® knock-knock jokes / by Mark Acey and Scott Nickel.
Description: Minneapolis : Lerner Publications, [2021] | Series: Garfield's ® belly laughs | Audience: Ages: 7–11 | Audience: Grades: 2–3 | Summary: "Who's there? It's Garfield, the fat cat! Laugh along with the best knock-knock jokes from this funny feline and his furry (and not so furry) friends. These jokes are sure to brighten up even the worst Monday!"– Provided by publisher.
Identifiers: LCCN 2019036582 (print) | LCCN 2019036583 (ebook) | ISBN 9781541589810 (library binding) | ISBN 9781728400242 (ebook)
Subjects: LCSH: Garfield (Fictitious character)—Juvenile literature. | Knock-knock jokes—Juvenile literature.
Classification: LCC PN6231.K55 N528 2021 (print) | LCC PN6231.K55 (ebook) | DDC 818/.602–dc23

LC record available at https://lccn.loc.gov/2019036582
LC ebook record available at https://lccn.loc.gov/2019036583

Manufactured in the United States of America
1-47491-48035-11/20/2019

KNOCK, KNOCK.

Who's there?
Ken.
Ken who?
Ken you come out and play?

KNOCK, KNOCK.

Who's there?
Harry.
Harry who?
Harry up and open
the door!

KNOCK, KNOCK.

Who's there?
Witch.
Witch who?
Witch you'd stop asking
questions and let me in!

KNOCK, KNOCK.
Who's there?
Anita.
Anita who?
Anita more food—here comes Garfield!

KNOCK, KNOCK.
Who's there?
Jimmy.
Jimmy who?
Jimmy some cake! I'm starving!

7

KNOCK, KNOCK.

Who's there?
Feline.
Feline who?
Feline blue because you won't let me in.

KNOCK, KNOCK.

Who's there?
G. I.
G. I. who?
G. I. wish you'd open the door!

KNOCK, KNOCK.

Who's there?
Aladdin.
Aladdin who?
Aladdin my class has a girlfriend named Jeannie.

KNOCK, KNOCK.

Who's there?
Juan.
Juan who?
Juan plus Juan equals two.

KNOCK, KNOCK.
Who's there?
Drew.
Drew who?
Drew a picture of
Garfield and Odie!

WE ALL KNOW
WHO'S THE
STAR OF THAT
PICTURE!

KNOCK, KNOCK.

Who's there?
Turnip.
Turnip who?
Turnip the music—my favorite song is playing!

KNOCK, KNOCK.

Who's there?
Mariah.
Mariah who?
Mariah arm is getting tired from all this knocking!

KNOCK, KNOCK.
Who's there?
York.
York who?
York cat just ate my bird!

KNOCK, KNOCK.
Who's there?
Phil.
Phil who?
Phil like ordering a pizza?

KNOCK, KNOCK.

Who's there?
Kareem.
Kareem who?
Kareem-filled cupcakes are Garfield's favorite!

KNOCK, KNOCK.

Who's there?
Marsha.
Marsha who?
Marsha-mallows! Get ready to roast!

KNOCK, KNOCK.

Who's there?
Phillip.
Phillip who?
Phillip my plate!

I ALWAYS WATCH WHAT I EAT . . . OTHERWISE, SOME CRUMBS MIGHT GET AWAY!

KNOCK, KNOCK.

Who's there?
Olive.
Olive who?
Olive chocolate. Don't you?

KNOCK, KNOCK.

Who's there?
Ida.
Ida who?
Ida the lasagna,
Garfield's coming!

KNOCK, KNOCK.

Who's there?
Jackie-Anne.
Jackie-Anne who?
Jackie-Anne Jilly
went up the hilly.

KNOCK, KNOCK.

Who's there?
Freddy.
Freddy who?
Freddy or not,
here I come!

THAT SOUNDS
LIKE A LOT
OF WORK

KNOCK, KNOCK.

Who's there?

Tom.

Tom who?

Tom for another "knock, knock" joke!

KNOCK, KNOCK.

Who's there?
Roach.
Roach who?
Roach you a letter, but you didn't answer.

KNOCK, KNOCK.

Who's there?
Leah.
Leah who?
Leah me alone.

KNOCK, KNOCK.

Who's there?
Candy.
Candy who?
Candy dog play
with de bone?

KNOCK, KNOCK.

Who's there?
Fido.
Fido who?
Fido know . . . I'm
just a dog!

KNOCK, KNOCK.

Who's there?
Ben.
Ben who?
Ben there. Done that.

THAT JOKE WAS ALMOST AS BAD AS MONDAYS

MONDAY

KNOCK, KNOCK.
Who's there?
You.
You who?
Well you-hoo
to you too!

KNOCK, KNOCK.
Who's there?
Audrey.
Audrey who?
Audrey enough, *I*
don't know either.

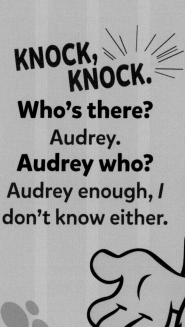

KNOCK, KNOCK.

Who's there?
Randy.
Randy who?
Randy marathon . . . and boy, am I pooped!

I MIGHT AS WELL EXERCISE . . . I'M IN A BAD MOOD ANYWAY

KNOCK, KNOCK.
Who's there?
Dragon.
Dragon who?
Dragon this big tail
around makes me tired!

KNOCK, KNOCK.

Who's there?
Gladys.
Gladys who?
Gladys summer!
Aren't you?

KNOCK, KNOCK.

Who's there?
Rob.
Rob who?
Rob some
sunblock on me
before I burn up!

KNOCK, KNOCK.
Who's there?
Linda.
Linda who?
Linda me a dollar
till Friday!

KNOCK, KNOCK.
Who's there?
Les.
Les who?
Les go crazy!

KNOCK, KNOCK.
Who's there?
Bill.
Bill who?
Bill you please stop asking these silly questions?!

KNOCK, KNOCK.
Who's there?
Candice.
Candice who?
Candice be the last "knock, knock" joke?

SEE YA LATER. I'VE GOT PLACES TO GO AND PEOPLE TO ANNOY!